INDIGENOUS AMERICAN CULTURES

Celebrating the APACHE

KIM THOMPSON

Mitchell Lane
PUBLISHERS

Parent and Caregiver Tips for Creating Nonfiction Readers

The high-interest topics in the ***Indigenous American Cultures*** series are sure to get your young reader excited about reading nonfiction. While exploring a fascinating subject, your reader will be introduced to new facts, ideas, and vocabulary.

Tips for Reading Nonfiction

Talk about Nonfiction

Explain that nonfiction books provide facts about real-world topics. When readers read nonfiction, they gain a rich understanding of the world. They build background knowledge that provides a foundation for learning and academic success.

Look at the Parts

This book contains the following helpful features. Share the purpose of each feature with your reader.

Photos, Captions, and Graphic Aids
The photos, captions, maps, diagrams, time lines, and other graphic aids in nonfiction texts contain a wealth of information. Help your reader identify different ways information can be displayed.

Sidebars
These extra tidbits of information help satisfy readers' curiosity and expand their knowledge.

Table of Contents
Located at the front of the book, this list shows the big ideas within the text and the page numbers where they can be found.

Glossary
Located at the back of the book, the glossary defines key words and phrases that are related to the topic. These words and phrases can be found in the text in colored type.

Comprehension Questions (Fact Check)
Multiple-choice questions help readers self-check to make sure they understand what they read.

Index
Located at the back of the book, the index is an alphabetical list of topics and the page numbers where they can be found.

With a little help and guidance, your reader will be on their way to enjoying and learning from nonfiction books.

Mitchell Lane
PUBLISHERS

mitchelllanepub.com

2001 SW 31st Avenue
Hallandale, FL 33009

First Edition, 2027.
Author: Kim Thompson
Designer: Rhea Magaro

Series: Indigenous American Cultures
Title: Celebrating the Apache / by Kim Thompson

Hallandale, FL : Mitchell Lane Publishers, [2027]

Library bound ISBN: 979-8-89260-915-9
Paperback ISBN: 979-8-90145-066-6
eBook ISBN: 979-8-90145-025-3

Library of Congress
Control Number: 2026930277

PHOTO CREDITS
Alamy: GpPhotoStudio, 1; Danita Delimont, 1; William Cushman, 11; Jesus Cervantes, 13; M L Pearson, 14; NPS, 20; Danita Delimont, 21; Anders Ryman, 22; RGB Ventures / SuperStock, 23; ZUMA Press, Inc., 24, 25; Ritzau, 26; Alpha Stock, 28; Public Domain: Amon Carter Museum of American Art, 8; Granger Meador, 17; Library of Congress, 5, 6, 7, 13, 16, 18; Midnight Beliver, 12; Portland Art Museum, 19; U.S. National Archives and Records Administration, 9; Wikipedia, 27; Shutterstock: 86Eric_Anthony_Mischke 86, 1; Heliumstring Studio, 1; Joseph Sohm, 15; Kit Leong, 24; HES Photography, 25; Laurens Hoddenbagh, 29.

CONTENTS

AN APACHE CONNECTION

Do you know the name Geronimo? You may have heard it in a song. You might have listened to someone yell it while jumping from a high place. You probably understand that the name suggests courage or daring. But you may not know much about the man it refers to.

In Spanish, *Geronimo* is the name of a saint. Mexicans may have shouted prayers to this saint when they were under attack by a fierce Apache warrior. His real name was Goyahkla, but the nickname stuck. With just a few followers, Geronimo fought thousands of soldiers who threatened his people.

Culture Close-Up

For a time, one-quarter of the entire United States Army was trying to capture Geronimo. In 1886, he became the last Native American leader to surrender.

APACHE HISTORY

About one thousand years ago, the Apache moved south into lands that are now parts of Arizona, Colorado, New Mexico, Texas, and Mexico. These **Indigenous** people were mostly **nomadic**.

The Apache lived in small groups, or bands. The strongest male leader was in charge of each band. Some bands joined together.

Apache bands hunted, farmed, and gathered wild foods. They traded with local tribes. Some warriors **raided** other tribes. They raided villages controlled by Spain and Mexico.

Culture Close-Up

In the 1600s, the Apache got horses from Spanish colonizers. They became masters at riding and breeding them.

American **settlers** wanted to mine for gold, silver, and coal on Apache land. They wanted to limit where Apache people could live. The Apache resisted. They wanted to be free.

From 1861 to 1886, the Apache were at war with the U.S. Army. Even though they were outnumbered, they made many successful raids. Finally, they were forced to surrender.

Culture Close-Up

Some Apache bands escaped to the Sierra Madre Mountains in northern Mexico. Their families live there today.

Some went to Oklahoma, where they were prisoners for many years. Others moved to **reservations** in the Southwest. Today, there are nearly 200,000 Apache people in the U.S. They belong to many tribes. Some are the San Carlos Apache Tribe, the White Mountain Apache Tribe, and the Jicarilla Apache Nation.

After surrender, Geronimo and his followers were put on trains and sent to prisons far away. Geronimo spent 23 years as a prisoner. He died as a prisoner in Fort Sill, Oklahoma.

EXPLORING APACHE PLACES

You can learn about the Apache by visiting Chiricahua National Monument in Arizona. In this **sacred** place, "standing rocks" tower above the desert.

Long ago, Apache people came to these heights to escape the summer heat. Cliffs and canyons helped them hide from enemies.

Culture Close-Up

Apache Pass is nearby. One of the biggest battles in the Apache Wars happened here. The great chief Cochise led an attack on the U.S. Army.

You can visit Fort Apache Historic Park in Arizona. Museum exhibits explain how Apache people lived long ago. You can peek inside **wickiups**. These traditional homes were built from willow branches, grasses, and other natural materials.

Culture Close-Up

Long ago, the Apache gathered wild plants for food and medicine. The agave plant was an important source of food.

APACHE LANGUAGES

Apache languages first developed in areas that are now Alaska and Canada. Some of them are Jicarilla Apache, Mescalero Apache, and Western Apache.

Not many people speak these languages well. The Fort Sill Apache Tribe is working to change this. They offer monthly language classes. Other tribes have created apps and dictionaries to help people learn their languages.

Culture Close-Up

Apache people call themselves *Nde*, which means "the people."

Culture Close-Up

Practice these Western Apache words.
ndeeń (man)
izdzán (woman)
góshé (dog)
ya'áí (sun)
tł'é'gona'áí (moon)

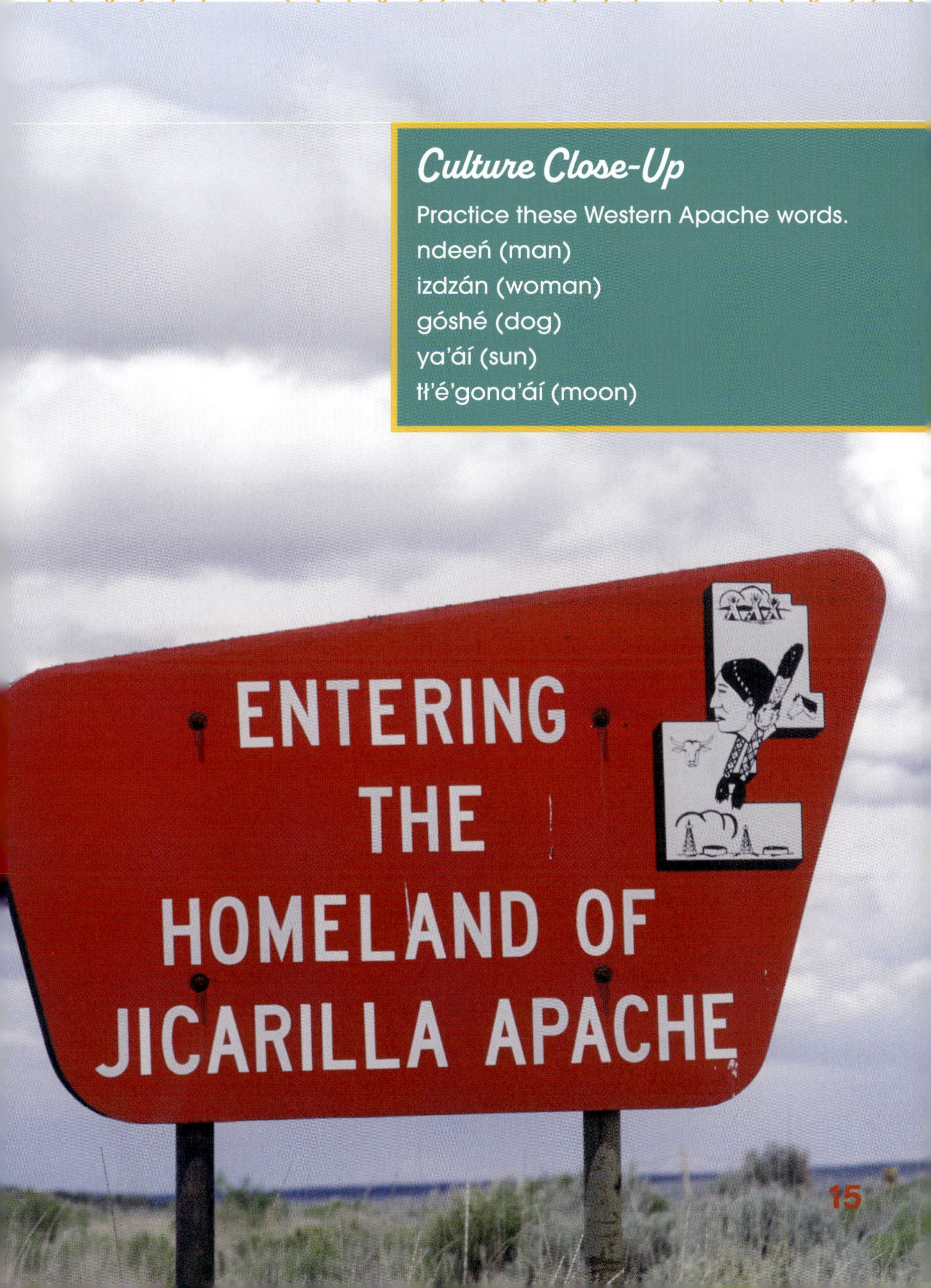

HONORING APACHE TRADITIONS

Long ago, Apache men were expert hunters and **guerrilla** warriors. At the age of eight, boys began their training. They studied plants, animals, seasons, and the land. As a test of strength, young men had to run for two days without stopping.

Warriors carried spears, knives, and clubs. They made wooden bows and arrows tipped with stone, bone, or metal.

Today, Apache people honor their warrior culture. Apache artist Allan Houser made the sculpture *Sacred Rain Arrow*. It stands outside a museum in Tulsa, Oklahoma.

Culture Close-Up

Once, the Apache hunted deer, antelope, rabbits, and other animals. Many hunted bison on the Great Plains. They used animal hides for clothing and shelter.

The Apache are known for making beautiful baskets and intricate bead designs. The skills are often passed from mother to daughter. Long ago, paints and dyes were made from plants and used to decorate clothing and other items.

Lynnette Haozous

Today, Apache artists honor their culture. Lynnette Haozous paints murals. Her work includes traditional Apache themes and designs.

Music and dance are important to the Apache. The Crown Dance or Mountain Spirit Dance is done to honor traditions and bring healing. Five male dancers wear black masks and tall crowns. Four of the dancers represent north, south, east, and west. The fifth is a clown who drives away evil spirits.

Apache people still perform this dance. It is a part of many festivals and celebrations.

The dancers do not talk to each other. They wave their sticks to communicate. As drums beat, the dancers whistle, shriek, and howl.

APACHE CELEBRATIONS

The Sunrise Ceremony is an important celebration for Apache girls who are becoming women. It lasts for several days and involves the whole community. There are songs, dances, prayers, and gifts. The girl wears a special dress and takes a new name. She is dusted with **pollen** as a blessing.

Culture Close-Up

Apache women have always held positions of power. After marriage, a man traditionally moves in with his wife's family.

Each year, Apache join people from many other tribes at the American Indian Expo in Oklahoma. There are art fairs, games, and carnival rides. Dancers compete for prizes. People eat fry bread and other traditional foods. During a parade, people wave to princesses riding on floats. One is crowned from each tribe.

FAMOUS FACES

Vincent Neil Emerson writes country music and plays guitar. Songs such as "The Ballad of the Choctaw-Apache" celebrate his **heritage**.

Mary Kim Titla is a member of the San Carlos Apache Tribe. She was one of the first Native American TV journalists. In 2008, she ran for Congress. She is the executive director of United National Indian Tribal Youth (UNITY).

Victorio

Culture Close-Up

Apache chiefs and leaders hold an important place in American history. They include Geronimo, Cochise, Victorio, and Mangas Coloradas.

LESSONS FROM THE APACHE

The Apache respect their elders and care for their children. They believe that animals and the land are sources of strength.

Modern Apache people lead ordinary modern lives. But they remember their past and celebrate their culture. Their traditions teach important lessons about honoring nature and community.

GLOSSARY

guerrilla (guh-RIL-uh): a style of warfare in which small groups of fighters battle larger forces by ambushing, raiding, and retreating to hidden places

heritage (HER-i-tij): traditions and beliefs that people consider to be an important part of their history

Indigenous (in-DI-juh-nuhs): the earliest known inhabitants of a place

nomadic (noh-MAD-ik): traveling from place to place instead of living in the same place all the time

pollen (PAH-luhn): a fine, yellow powder that is made by flowers and that helps corn and other plants reproduce

raided (RAY-did): attacked suddenly and surprisingly to hurt enemies and often to steal; during raids, the Apache might have taken food, horses, weapons, and other items

reservations (rez-ur-VAY-shuhnz): areas of land set aside by the government for ownership by an Indigenous American tribe

sacred (SAY-krid): holy, very important, and deserving of great respect

settlers (SET-luhrz): people who make their homes in a new place and who have historically invaded and oppressed Indigenous peoples who originally lived there

wickiups (WI-key-uhps): small, domed shelters with rough wood frames covered by grass mats and animal hides; wickiups were easy to take down and put up, helping the Apache travel from place to place

FACT CHECK

1. Geronimo was ________.

   A. a saint B. an Apache leader C. an American settler

2. During a raid, the Apache _______.

   A. danced B. built shelters C. attacked enemies

3. Many Apache people lived _______.

   A. in the desert B. near the ocean C. in Canada

4. The Crown Dance features ______.

   A. pollen B. masks C. a parade

Answers: 1. B, 2. C, 3. A, 4. B

FURTHER READING

Bodden, Valerie. *Apache (First Peoples)*. Creative Education, 2018.

O'Brien, Cynthia. *Encyclopedia of American Indian History and Culture*. National Geographic Kids, 2019.

ON THE INTERNET

Mescalero Apache Tribe
mescaleroapachetribe.com
Explore the official website of one Apache tribe.

Native Hope: What Happened to the Apache Tribe?
blog.nativehope.org/history-of-the-apache-nation
Read facts, past and present, about a great Indigenous nation.

Vice Media: Inside an Apache Rite of Passage into Womanhood
youtube.com/watch?v=r1Cx_9YDQEc
Follow one Apache girl as she and her family journey through the Sunrise Ceremony.

INDEX

ABOUT THE AUTHOR

Kim Thompson has written more than one hundred books for young readers. She is a fan of American history and loves digging deep to explore stories from the past. Kim thinks it's important to remember ancestors and keep cultural traditions alive. She's grateful for the privilege and adventure of writing this book.